Cambridge **Discovery Education**™

▶ **INTERACTIVE READERS**

Series editor: Bob Hastings

LIFT OFF
EXPLORING THE UNIVERSE

B2+

Caroline Shackleton and Nathan Paul Turner

CAMBRIDGE
UNIVERSITY PRESS

32 Avenue of the Americas, New York, NY 10013-2473, USA

Cambridge University Press is part of the University of Cambridge.

It furthers the University's mission by disseminating knowledge in the pursuit of education, learning and research at the highest international levels of excellence.

www.cambridge.org
Information on this title: www.cambridge.org/9781107692497

First published 2014
5th printing 2015

Printed in Hong Kong, China, by Golden Cup Printing Company Limited

A catalogue record for this publication is available from the British Library

Library of Congress Cataloging-in-Publication Data

Shackleton, Caroline.
  Lift off : exploring the universe / Caroline Shackleton and Nathan Paul Turner.
    pages cm. — (Cambridge discovery interactive readers)
  ISBN 978-1-107-69249-7 (pbk. : alk. paper)
  1. Outer space—Juvenile literature. 2. English language—Textbooks for foreign speakers.
  3. Readers (Elementary) I. Title.

TL793.S417 2013
919.904—dc23

                                  2013023924

ISBN 978-1-107-69249-7

Additional resources for this publication at www.cambridge.org

Layout services, art direction, book design, and photo research: Q2ABillSMITH GROUP
Editorial services: Hyphen S.A.
Audio production: CityVox, New York
Video production: Q2ABillSMITH GROUP

Contents

Before You Read:
Get Ready!

Space travel is dangerous and expensive, but many people are prepared to risk their lives to travel in space.

Words to Know

Complete the definitions with the correct words.

astronaut   colonize   galaxy   solar system   space probe

1 _____ : a sun and the group of planets that move around it

2 _____ : send people to live in a new place, such as the planet Mars

3 _____ : a person who is trained for traveling in spaceships

4 _____ : one of the large, independent groups of stars in the universe

5 _____ : a small spaceship, with no one traveling in it, sent into space to get information and send it back to scientists on Earth

Words to Know

Read the paragraph. Then complete the definitions below with the correct highlighted words.

The early history of space flight begins with the question of how to launch a spaceship so that it goes fast enough to break free of the field of gravity, which holds everything to the surface of the planet. A ship needs to travel at the speed of 40,320 km/h, known as escape velocity, to reach a distance where gravity is not strong enough to pull it back down to Earth, but is strong enough to keep the ship floating in orbit around the planet. The first man-made object to reach escape velocity was the Russian Luna 1 in January 1959. It was not a manned flight, however. Luna 1 only carried radio equipment and scientific instruments. The first manned mission was two years later, when Yuri Gagarin became the first person to travel in space.

1 _____: the force that makes objects fall toward the Earth

2 _____: carrying people

3 _____: the curved path that objects in space follow around a planet or star

4 _____: send something out, especially a vehicle into space

5 _____: the outer or top part of something

6 _____: sending someone to a place to do a particular job, or the job itself

Video Quest

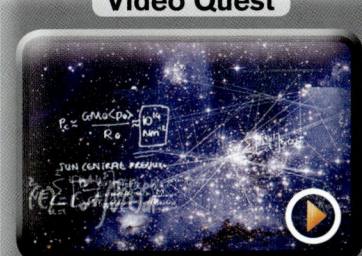

What Is the Universe?

Watch this video about the universe and find out how scientists make predictions about the part of the universe we cannot see. How can they do this?

CHAPTER 1

What's Out There?

ZHEE STARED THROUGH THE WINDOW AT THE SPACEPORT RISING UP OUT OF THE ORANGE RAIN-GAS CLOUDS BELOW. SHE HAD NEVER SEEN SUCH NOISE AND FILTH.[1]...

In five minutes the ship she was traveling on would touch down in the middle of Shangha-port, one of the busiest spaceports still operating on Old Terra. A funny feeling, this homecoming that wasn't.

Zhee knew that she had been born on Old Terra, Earth, one of the last of her work-group, before their section was sent up to Moonblock 9. Not that they'd stayed long on the moon. Zhee was still a baby when her group had moved to Mars after the '65 discovery of uranium[2] on the red planet. Since then, Zhee had spent most of her 94 years working the rich mines on Mars's unwelcoming surface, going on vacation to the pleasure-ships in orbit above.

[1] **filth:** a lot of dirt
[2] **uranium:** a heavy metal that is used in the production of nuclear power

The long-ago memory of green Old Terra remained strong in most people's minds, though, and when news had come through of special return permits for a new ecology project that was under way in Sahara, the desert continent, Zhee had jumped at the chance. She'd worked in Mars's terrible conditions for 70 years now, so she imagined she could cope with a bit of Old Terra desert, no matter what people said.

If the project went well, they would take the new technology back to Mars and create a second, more fertile[3] Earth. Looking at the orange storm below, Zhee had to admit that Earth was not what she had imagined . . .

We have no way of knowing whether the future of space exploration will be anything like Zhee's experience, or where present space exploration may lead us, but experiments with living in and exploring space have been going on for over 50 years.

[3] **fertile:** (of land) able to produce a large number of high-quality plants

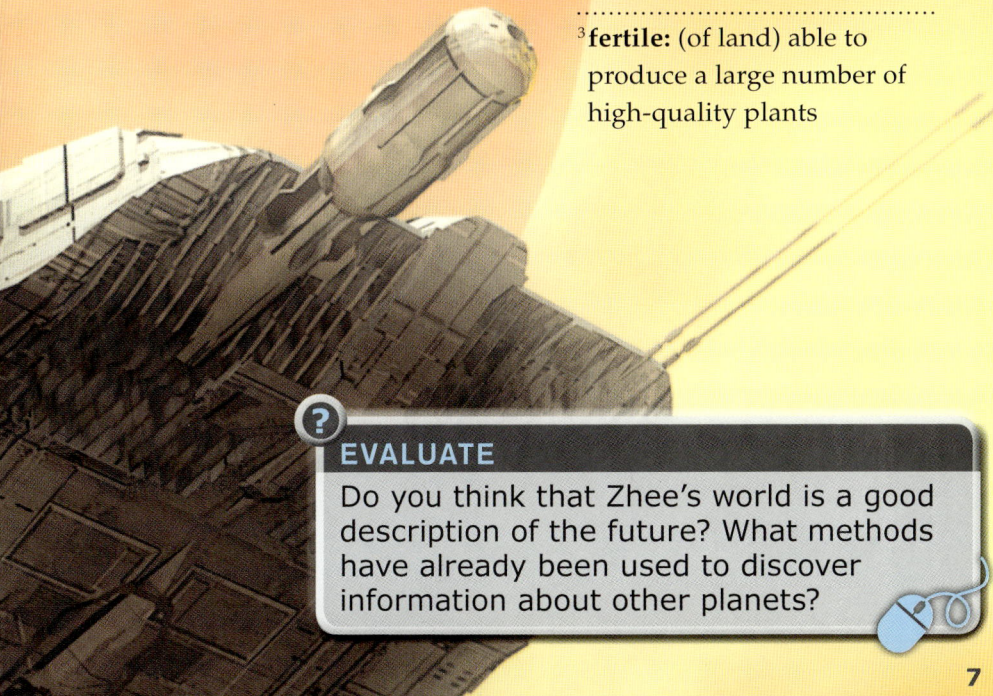

?

EVALUATE

Do you think that Zhee's world is a good description of the future? What methods have already been used to discover information about other planets?

The beginnings of space exploration are tied to the Cold War, when political competition between the Soviet Union and the United States moved up into space. Many early achievements were Russian, such as the first rocket to orbit the Earth (1957), the first astronaut (Yuri Gagarin, 1961), and the first woman in space (Valentina Tereshkova, 1963). The USA responded with its Apollo program, which eventually sent Neil Armstrong to become the first man on the moon, in 1969.

By the 1970s, however, cooperation was beginning to replace competition, as political relations improved. This led to projects such as the 1998 launch of the International Space Station, to this date the longest-inhabited space station.

Manned spaceflights are still limited to the exosphere, the highest level of the Earth's atmosphere. No human has ever gone further than our moon, and manned flights to more distant destinations, such as the planet Mars, are still not possible.

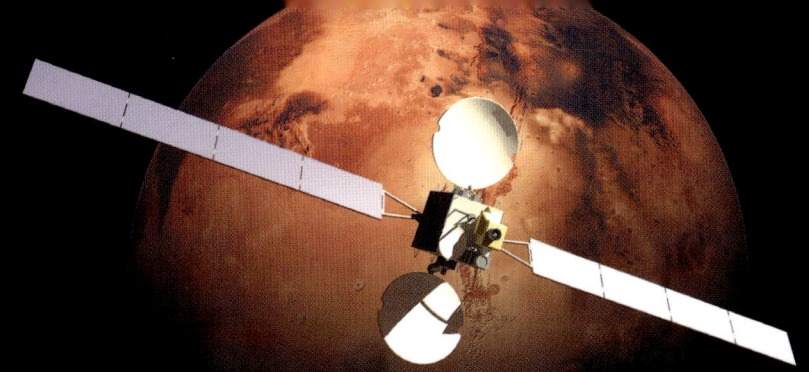

However, the use of unmanned space probes has a very successful history. These missions are mostly fact-finding missions, but they are also used to test space-flight technology for later use in manned flights. They can be either orbiters, which take photos from space, or landers, which take information from the planet's surface. Much of what we now know about our neighboring planets, for example the existence of ice on Mars, has come from successful probe explorations.

Rovers are unmanned vehicles that are used to explore planetary surfaces. They have the advantage of being mobile, which means they can travel around and send back information about many areas of a planet. Several countries have successfully landed rovers on Mars. Presently the USA has a rover, *Curiosity*, exploring the planet. The information these missions send back may one day allow manned missions to Mars.

Video Quest

Life on Mars?

Watch this video about Mars. What do scientists want to know about Mars? What method are they using to find answers?

CHAPTER 2

At Home in Space

FOR HUMANS TO CONTINUE TO EXPLORE OUR GALAXY, THE MILKY WAY, WE WILL NEED TO BE ABLE TO LIVE IN SPACE FOR LONG PERIODS OF TIME.

Living long-term in a low-gravity or micro-gravity environment like space can have harmful effects on the human body. It can make movement difficult, weaken muscles and bone, and cause changes in our immune system,[4] vision, and taste. Although scientists have learned how to solve these problems through exercise, diet, and medicines, astronauts who spend long periods of time in micro-gravity conditions still find they are very weak when they return to Earth's higher gravity.

So far, the record for the longest time spent outside of Earth's atmosphere is held by the Russian astronaut Valeri Polyakov, who stayed on the space station Mir for about 14 months to test effects on the human body. Returning to Earth, Polyakov managed to walk from his spaceship to a chair, to the amazement of everyone there. That same day he is rumored to have said, "We can fly to Mars."

[4] **immune system:** the body's cells and organs that fight illness and disease

Polyakov's experiences showed that astronauts could spend long periods of time in space without suffering long-term problems, although there are still questions about whether humans could live for many years in this kind of environment.

Living in space provides other challenges. Space is almost a vacuum,[5] with neither the pressure[6] nor oxygen to support the human body. The low pressure causes swelling[7] and also a drop in blood temperature. Humans exposed to a vacuum would lose **consciousness** almost immediately, and **exposure** of more than 90 seconds is deadly. However, the effects are not as dramatic as some Hollywood movies would have us believe, and experiments on animals show strong recovery from exposure of less than 90 seconds.

[5]**vacuum:** a space without any gas or other matter in it, or a space from which most of the air or gas has been removed
[6]**pressure:** force caused by one thing pushing against another thing
[7]**swelling:** become larger and fuller

Living and working in space requires special suits and pressurized cabins. A major challenge for astronauts is the low-gravity, or micro-gravity environment, which means they must re-learn how to move the body. In this environment, it is as if the body is weightless. In fact, everything floats, even liquids!

Of course, this makes normal daily activities such as eating, drinking, and washing much more complicated to do without special equipment. Astronauts often sleep tied into special beds so they do not hurt themselves while they are unconscious. To prepare themselves for this environment, astronauts spend months training underwater.

The record for the farthest manned flight was set by the US spacecraft Apollo 13 in 1970 when it went around the far side of the moon, reaching a distance of about 321,868 kilometers from Earth. However, there have been many plans to travel farther.

Due to its closeness to Earth, its dramatic red color, and the fact that it's a terrestrial[8] planet, Mars has long been a subject of fascination for both scientists and science-fiction writers. Nineteenth-century questions about the possibility of life on Mars turned into 20th–century theories of possible human **colonization** of the planet. These theories became more realistic once probes had confirmed there is ice on Mars.

There have been numerous government as well as private **proposals** for a manned mission to Mars. Based on probe missions, it is estimated the journey would take 150–300 days, depending on the orbits of Earth and Mars, and the amount of **fuel** used. Given the long time frame, some experts including Buzz Aldrin, the second man on the moon, have suggested that these missions be permanent colonizations. This proposal has become known as "Mars to Stay."

[8]**terrestrial:** a rocky planet like the Earth

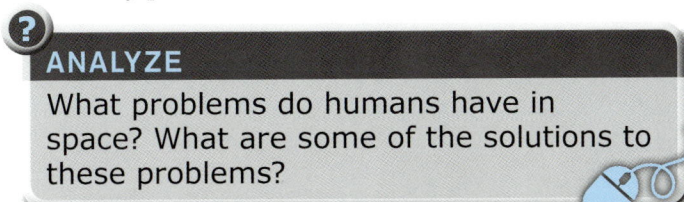

ANALYZE

What problems do humans have in space? What are some of the solutions to these problems?

CHAPTER 3

What Lies Beyond?

COULD MARS ONE DAY BE A SECOND EARTH?

While there are many different proposals for the next stage of human space exploration, most experts agree that the next logical stage is the exploration of Mars. There are presently three major proposals for how this should be achieved.

Some think we should first set up a base on the moon from which to send missions onwards to Mars. Another option would be to send regular, short-term missions to Mars to experiment with living there. However, a much more adventurous option has been proposed to colonize the planet directly.

Mars One, a private Dutch company, proposes to set up a colony on Mars by 2023, sending in new ships of four colonists every two years.

One of the ways they aim to pay for this project is by selling TV rights, as a kind of Space Colony Reality TV! While the project has opponents, some experts insist that it is possible with today's technology.

The Mars One project claims to have two advantages:

- Simplicity. They only plan to use tried and tested technology that is already available.

- One-way trips. They do not intend to return any of the colonists to Earth! With a no-return flight they wouldn't need extra fuel to get off Mars, and their colony wouldn't require expensive technology like nuclear reactors.[9] Instead, they could get the power they need from solar panels.[10]

Mars One began the selection of the astronauts in 2013. Whether they will receive the six billion dollars they would need remains to be seen, but it is one example of the seriousness with which people are looking at space exploration.

[9]**nuclear reactor:** a large machine that produces nuclear energy
[10]**solar panel:** a device that changes energy from the sun into electricity

Going deeper into space is presently impossible for manned flights. The distances involved are simply too great for ships to successfully support human life.

Our solar system has a radius[11] of billions of kilometers. How long would it take to cross such an enormous distance? Well, in fact we already know the answer due to the amazing journey of two robotic probes, Voyager 1 and Voyager 2.

Launched within weeks of each other in 1977, each Voyager has been traveling in a different direction through the solar system at approximately 500 million kilometers per year. They brought us the first pictures of Saturn and Neptune and are now reaching the limits of the solar system. So far, the journey has taken them 35 years. Obviously such a journey for humans would be a voyage of no return, and is presently impossible without a way of producing the necessary air, food, and equipment on the spaceship.

[11] **radius:** (the length of) a straight line from the center of a circle to its edge

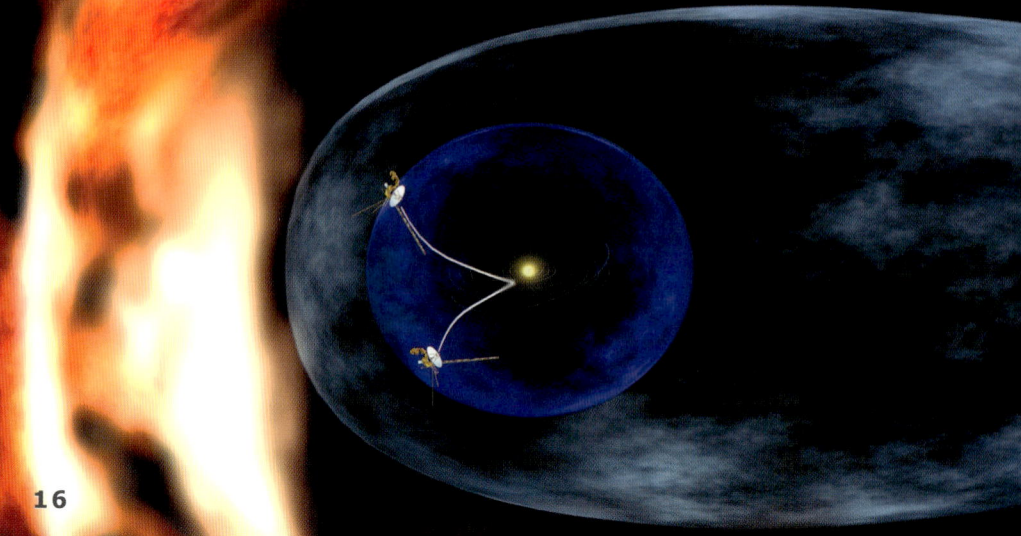

Beyond the limits of the solar system, we can only watch from a distance. Not that this technology is any less impressive. Since the beginnings of astronomy scientists have been constantly improving telescopes and space observatories[12] to better understand the universe. The latest and most powerful telescope is the Hubble, a space telescope launched into orbit above the Earth in 1990.

The Hubble Space Telescope

Using the Hubble telescope, scientists have gained great understanding of the nature of the universe, such as its present

A black hole

rate of **expansion**. Other important Hubble discoveries have been the confirmation of black holes at the centers of nearby galaxies, as well as important information that has helped scientists with new theories of dark matter, the material thought to make up most of the known universe.

[12]**observatory:** a building equipped for studying the planets and the stars

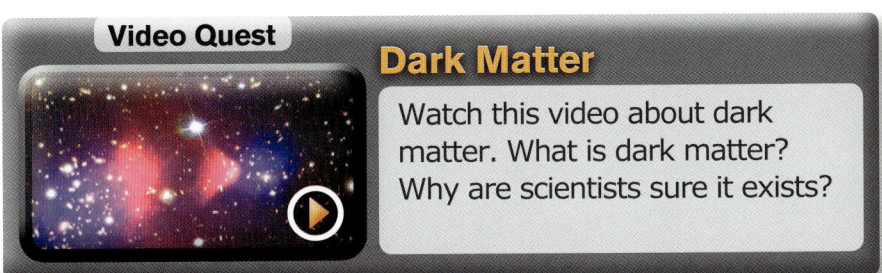

Video Quest

Dark Matter

Watch this video about dark matter. What is dark matter? Why are scientists sure it exists?

CHAPTER 4

Sci-Fi

"FANTASY IS THE IMPOSSIBLE MADE PROBABLE. SCIENCE FICTION IS THE IMPROBABLE MADE POSSIBLE." ROD SERLING, SCIENCE FICTION AUTHOR.

Humans have been fascinated with space since long before we knew how to get there. In 1865, the French writer Jules Verne published a novel about three men who traveled in a spaceship to the moon. Just over one hundred years later, the USA successfully sent its three-man Apollo 11 spaceship to the surface of the moon. Life had copied art.

Verne is a clear example of how human imagination can **inspire** people to very real technological achievements. The Russian scientist Konstantin Tsiolkovsky, one of the first and most important astrophysics scientists, claimed he was originally inspired by reading Verne's stories.

At the end of the 19th century there were incredible technological advances and wonderful new inventions. With the birth of cinema in the early 20th century, Hollywood began a love affair with space travel and science fiction, which continues to this day. Many early science fiction novels, such as H.G. Wells' *The War of the Worlds*, were later made into films and shown on the big screen with amazing special effects for the time. Then, original science-fiction stories made it to the big screen.

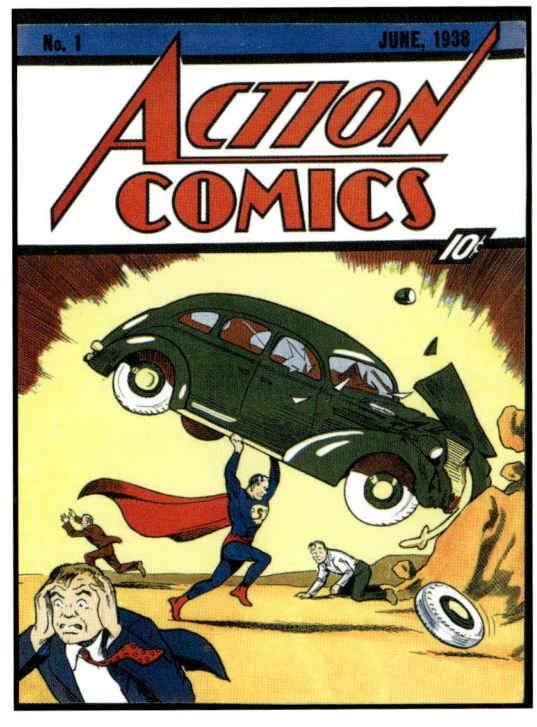

These movies helped create a new consciousness about the possibilities of space travel and of life beyond our own planet.

In 1938, writer Jerry Siegel and artist Joe Shuster's comic book *Superman* was published. The hero, an alien from another planet, quickly captured the nation's imagination. Soon the comic became a radio series and then in 1948, Superman went to Hollywood. Since then, nine Superman movies have been made, most recently *Man of Steel* in 2013.

Stanley Kubrik's 1968 movie *2001: A Space Odyssey*, based on the short story "The Sentinel" by Arthur C. Clarke, has become an all-time classic. The movie explores many classic sci-fi topics, such as the nature of consciousness, artificial intelligence, our ethics[13] toward machines, human origins, and our future role in the galaxy. Of course, the film is also essentially about space, and about the fear and fascination we have with what lies beyond the limits of our own world.

At the time Kubrik was making *2001*, both the American and Russian space programs were well under way. Although humans had not yet set foot on the moon, there had been a number of manned space flights, some of which had sent photographs of Earth back to people at home. For the first time, people knew what Earth looked like from space, and also just how small and delicate our world really is.

[13] **ethics:** a set of beliefs about what is right and wrong

An alien

By the 1970s there were many movies and television series about space travel. Many had one thing in common; human exploration of new worlds. From *Star Trek* and *Battlestar Galactica*, set in the future, to *Star Wars*, set a "long, long time ago, in a galaxy far, far away . . .," humans were the stars of the show. And yet, our idea of aliens was changing, too.

Previously, aliens had been monstrous, insect-like creatures who threatened to destroy humanity. When Hollywood director Orson Welles made a version of *War of the Worlds* for radio in 1938, thousands of people listening believed Earth was actually being invaded by creatures from Mars – Martians! A terrible panic broke out as people tried to escape from cities across the USA. But now a more complicated view of aliens was taking shape. *Star Wars* thrilled us with the wealth of its worlds, its religious and political systems, and above all its alien characters, who were just as likely to be our friends as they were our enemies.

Star Trek, one of the longest-running and most popular sci-fi series of all time, seemed to represent everything that most fascinates us about science fiction, with its small group of human travelers exploring strange new planets, amazed by the alien cultures they find there.

Star Trek seems to be a winning recipe. It is particularly famous for the obsessive character of its fans, known as Trekkies, who spend fortunes on *Star Trek* souvenirs and on attending special conferences.

What is it about sci-fi shows like *Star Trek* that fires people's imaginations? Perhaps there is something that calls to our need for exploration, for new experiences and unexplored frontiers.[14] With the whole Earth now mapped, space truly is, in the words of *Star Trek*'s Captain Kirk, "the final frontier."

[14] **frontier:** a border between what is known and what is not known

While we may have a hunger for exploring these new frontiers, at the moment sci-fi seems the only way of satisfying it. Present space technology is light years behind the expectations of readers and viewers, who are used to long-distance space travel, intelligent robots, and teleportation.[15] Although we have put a man on the moon, we are still some years away from sending manned flights to the nearest planet, Mars, and anything farther away seems impossible.

And yet, the history of science fiction shows us that humans are remarkably creative, able to take possibilities from today's technology and imagine new situations beyond present scientific understanding. Carl Sagan's *Contact*, for example, introduces the possibility of using wormholes[16] in space to travel huge distances in time, allowing humans to get around the limitations of rocket-powered travel.

Who knows? The science fiction you see on the movie screen or read in a comic book today may one day become scientific fact.

....

[15] **teleportation:** travel using an imaginary super-fast form of transport that needs special technology or special mental powers

[16] **wormholes:** a type of space tunnel that some scientists think might connect parts of space and time

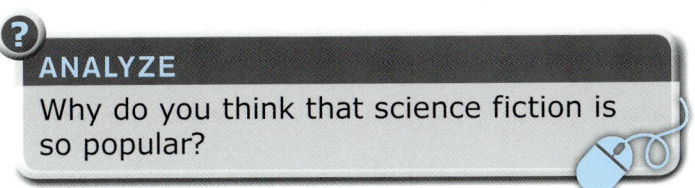

?

ANALYZE

Why do you think that science fiction is so popular?

CHAPTER 5

What Do You Think?

WE NOW HAVE THE TECHNOLOGICAL MEANS TO START COLONIZING NEARBY SPACE, BUT SHOULD WE?

The human population is rising fast. It is predicted to reach nine billion by 2050. This will severely threaten the natural environment. Many people argue, therefore, that space colonization is an urgent necessity. Others are not so sure. Take a look at some of the arguments for and against colonization and decide what you think.

Against: The current costs of space exploration are too high. The money could be much better spent here on Earth.

For: We know that the smallest asteroid[17] near Earth has more metals than humans have mined in their whole history. And on the asteroid Eros, there is more silver, gold, and aluminum than could ever be dug from the earth. Exploring space will give us all the natural resources we need.

. . . .

[17] **asteroid:** an object like a very large rock that goes around the sun like a planet

Against: The wars and conflicts we see on Earth will only get worse if we expand into space. We should concentrate on creating political unity here before we think about traveling into space.

For: Space exploration will create a sense of unity about our origins and humanity that we now lack. The present level of cooperation on the International Space Station shows that governments can learn to work together and to see the greater good.

Against: We are using up our natural resources. We have to reduce industrial production to save our natural environment. Space technology will only worsen our situation.

For: Moving our industrial production into space is the only way to ensure our survival and the protection of our environment. The future colonization of Mars could also provide a new environment for our huge population to live on.

After You Read

Read the sentences and choose Ⓐ, Ⓑ, Ⓒ, or Ⓓ.

1 What did Zhee think when she saw the planet where she was born?

Ⓐ It was exactly how she believed it to be.

Ⓑ It was very different from her expectations.

Ⓒ It was extremely crowded.

Ⓓ It was a good place for a vacation.

2 What are unmanned spaceships used for?

Ⓐ to make repairs to existing space stations

Ⓑ to take equipment to be used by astronauts

Ⓒ to send back photographs from the moon

Ⓓ to discover information about distant planets

3 What do astronauts have to do in preparation for their time in space?

Ⓐ read science-fiction stories

Ⓑ sleep in a special bed

Ⓒ train in special conditions

Ⓓ wear special clothes

4 Why is living on Mars now a real possibility?

Ⓐ Frozen water has been found on Mars.

Ⓑ Sci-fi authors have suggested it was going to happen.

Ⓒ Buzz Aldrin says it can be done.

Ⓓ Animal experiments show it is possible.

5 What was unusual about the sci-fi radio program *War of the Worlds*?

Ⓐ A producer used alien characters.

Ⓑ A scientist developed ideas from the program.

Ⓒ People thought aliens were really attacking.

Ⓓ It was about a strange world in the future.

6 How did Carl Sagan imagine humans might be able to travel farther in space?

- (A) using a rocket
- (B) using special tunnels
- (C) using teleportation
- (D) using their imagination

7 What is the main argument for the colonization of other planets?

- (A) We naturally feel the need to explore space.
- (B) Governments want to become more powerful.
- (C) There will soon be too many people on Earth.
- (D) Governments could become rich by finding gold.

Complete the Text

Use the words in the box to complete the sci-fi story.

| alien | asteroid | astronaut | galaxy | observatory |

The President took a deep breath. She knew she wanted to be anywhere but here. However, she hadn't once thought of refusing the call from Professor Phobos to come to the famous Phobos

1 _____ .

In the building, people in white coats hurried toward her, but she ignored them, and stared at the bodies floating in the cool blue fluid in the center of the hall. "Not dead then . . ." she whispered.

"Not dead, no." replied the professor. "They could have floated across the whole **2** _____ for all we know. The ship is like nothing we've ever seen. We would never have seen it if it hadn't hit that **3** _____ ."

The president looked at him and turned back to the glass wall in front of her. She shook her head in complete disbelief. As an ex- **4** _____ , she had always imagined that one day they would find evidence of **5** _____ life, but the reality was almost unbelievable.

What happens next? Make up your own ending.

Answer Key

Words to Know, page 4

1 solar system **2** colonize **3** astronaut **4** galaxy
5 space probe

Words to Know, page 5

1 gravity **2** manned **3** orbit **4** launch **5** surface
6 mission

Video Quest, page 5

They make guesses. What they can see is regular, so they apply this to what they cannot see, and they think it will be the same.

Evaluate, page 7   *Answers will vary.*

Video Quest, page 9

They want to know if there is or has been life on Mars. They sent a robot geologist to find water.

Analyze, page 13   *Answers will vary.*

Video Quest, page 17

Scientists are not sure what it is made of, but they think it makes up 23 percent of all matter. They know it exists because they can measure its strong force of gravity, which they believe keeps galaxies together.

Analyze, page 23   *Answers will vary.*

Choose the Correct Answers, page 26

1 B **2** D **3** C **4** A **5** C **6** B **7** C

Complete the Text, page 27

1 Observatory **2** galaxy **3** asteroid **4** astronaut **5** alien